THE DOOR

THE DOOR
A Welcoming Entrance to Individual Light Verse

Elizabeth Stanley-Mallett

ARTHUR H. STOCKWELL LTD
Torrs Park   Ilfracombe   Devon
Established 1898
www.ahstockwell.co.uk

British Library Cataloguing-in-Publication Data.
A catalogue record for this book is available
from the British Library.

Previously published poems by the same author:
Guiding Star – Forward Press, 2009
Winter Sun – Forward Press, 2009
Beneath Rose-Lemon Skies – Arthur H. Stockwell Ltd, 2009
A Narrow By-Way – Anchor Books, 2010
Valentine – Forward Press, 2010
June Roses – Forward Press, 2010
Little Green Men – Forward Press, 2010
Before the Rainbow Fades Part II – Arthur H. Stockwell Ltd, 2010
Between Night and Dancing Light Part II – Arthur H. Stockwell Ltd, 2010
Valentine 2010 – Forward Poetry, 2011
Three to a Seat – Forward Poetry, 2011
Learners All – Forward Poetry, 2011

ISBN 978-0-7223-4119-3 Paperback edition.
ISBN 978-0-7223-4120-9 Cloth-bound edition.
Printed in Great Britain by
Arthur H. Stockwell Ltd
Torrs Park   Ilfracombe
Devon

PREFACE

Elizabeth Stanley-Mallett is foremost a woman's poet. Not of the classical or of today's modernist school, yet her work is contemporary with a touch of traditionalism.

Elizabeth produces light verse in which she describes her observations and views of life, on diverse subjects and themes.

Her poems have been previously published in various journals, e.g. Forward Press books of poetry etc. In the past she has collaborated with her husband, in producing three volumes of poetry. These books were published by Arthur H. Stockwell Ltd of Devon. The current book, *The Door*, is the first volume that is solely her own work.

Keith Stanley-Mallett

All poems are original and previously unpublished.

A Welcoming Entrance to Individual Light Verse

By

Elizabeth Stanley-Mallett

CONTENTS

Come Fresh April

April, the fourth month of the year
  Dispelling the winter's gloom,
Bird song fills the warmer air
Fragrant flowers burst into bloom.

The herald of springtime
  Good news for one and all.
April's magic is needed
In every home, hearth and hall.

Young creatures of diverse kind
  Growing so rapidly,
The product of Mother Nature
And April's great bounty.

It's glad we are April's here
  To bring a greater joy,
The spirit of nature joined
In living artful ploy.

Spirits lifted and warmer clime
  Inspiration for forward surge,
Building houses, planting seeds
April brings the urge.

Cooking

As I cook in the kitchen
Is it pleasure or a chore?
Making food for the family
    To spit out or ask for more.

Will they gulp it down
Or throw it down the sink?
Savoury aromas swiftly leaving
    A lingering nasty stink.

Good plain cooking wins the day
Yorkshire pudding and the roast,
It soon becomes a contest
    To see who eats the most.

Puddings, crumbles apple pie
Tempt the jaded palette,
The pastry is too hard to bite
    Must hit it with a mallet.

I feel I want to quit the scene
But I'm loath to give it up,
No fear of a great stampede
    To do the washing up?

Valentine 2010

Two lonely persons, two shattered lives
  Nothing left, and nothing to do,
No hopes, no dreams, no will to live
  Trancelike, stumbling, drifting through.

At last, one day in June
  A phone call, out of the blue,
A meeting – two hearts awoke
  And found new love – 'twas me and you.

To live again and fall in love
  A deep, enduring passion, strong,
That salved away the lonely years
  The solitary exile having gone.

My husband, true, we've been through hell
  Life has dealt us a bitter blow,
To each other we're still young
  Full of verve, get up and go.

Each year I write a few short lines
  To say how much I value you,
A love like ours transcends all time
  Wondrous, warm, and shining through.

Once Upon a Wishing Mood

Once upon a wishing mood
I allowed myself to wish,
Of castles large and knights of old
An imagined life of bliss.

Just to get away, from the daily grind,
Mundane chores and work in house,
I dreamt of being whisked away
Fondly, by a loving spouse.

Reality seemed so hard to bare
With pleasant days forsook,
I knew not of con man's tricks
Nor other kind of crooks.

Naïve to the point of ignorance
I filled my life with dross,
Rolling on in my silly way
My stone gathered no moss.

Maturity brought a little more sense
I learned not to wish too much,
Appreciate what I already had
And not at straws to clutch.

The Cuckoo

A visitor from overseas
    Noisy bandit of a bird,
That takes over another's nest
    Hedge-sparrows preferred.

Turfing out the resident eggs
    And depositing its own,
The poor duped foster mother
    Still squats upon her home.

Weeks pass, the egg hatches
    The cuckoo chick is there,
Fed by the foster birds
    No siblings left to share.

A greedy growing bird
    Its own parent away,
Comes the time to leave the nest
    And fly far south, each day.

Until a hotter land is reached
    Where adult birds abound,
Where It finds a mate to climb
    Back on the merry go round.

The Wastepaper Bin

A small receptacle under a desk
Usually overfull and spilling,
Onto the floor below, a mess
    Until the cleaner is willing –

To empty the small into a larger
Bits of paper all screwed round,
Confidential hours of work
    All in the bin are found.

Very handy for industrial spies
To retrieve such information,
And sell to a competitor
    For cash compensation.

Do not be careless with the waste
Shred confidential papers,
Make them useless for the spy
    Frustrating all his capers.

So keep the paper bin
Free from prying eyes,
Destroy your sensitive work
    That on the floor now lies.

Better still don't waste the paper
With multi-efforts all the same,
Get it right before printing out
    As all copy bears your name.

To Touch a Rainbow

A shimmering blend of colours rich
The shining arc spans the sky,
No matter how hard I reach
    I fail to touch it – why?

Falling to earth so far away
A band of exquisite hues,
Promising brighter weather
    A herald with good news.

Illusive, gleaming, illuminating
Seeming to touch the ground,
Where the rainbow falls is seen
    An enchanting treasure is found.

Imagination sees the rainbow as
A wondrous gift from on high,
To be appreciated by all who view
    This fleeting image in the sky.

Why cant it be touched or felt?
Is it really there at all?
Breaking up the clouds of storm
    With a rainbow's magic to enthral.

Treading the Boards

The comedian telling funny jokes
Does his best to entertain,
Has them rolling in the aisles
Or cringing down in pain.

Slapstick is great for the kids,
With water splashed everywhere,
Soaking clowns and helpers
And no one seems to care.

An actor paces the wooden stage
Afraid to fluff his lines,
He's bullied by the producer
Again, time after time.

So he nervously treads the boards
Backwards, forwards, up and down,
He loves the life in theatre-land
And he seeks to wear the crown –

The accolade of the major role
The leading man in future plays,
He trips over the props on stage
Now wants to slink away.

Yet, if by chance he makes it
And sees his name in lights,
It is as if an angel
Has helped, through all those nights.

Rehearsal after rehearsal
Fluffing so many of his lines
Yet all has come to fruition
He's now an actor of the times.

The Gossips

A group of old women
    Who from days of old,
Have spread malicious gossip
    Were labelled then as scolds.

They relished the demise of others
    Enjoyed their bad fate,
Relationships that grew too fast
    Love turning into hate.

The herbs and potions of some
    Had developed into an art,
But spells and magic soon became
    Unwanted, dangerous, part –

Of play to seek control
    Of simple country folk.
The gossips were made to rue
    The incantations they spoke.

The ducking stool awaited them
    To see if they would float,
In the village pond so deep
    A scared, handy scapegoat.

The pleasure they had taken
    In the problems of poor peers,
Would come back to haunt them
    For many tortured years.

The Buttercross

A simple means of selling wares
 Was the old Buttercross
Folk came from miles around
 To vend for profit or loss.

Just a crude stone monument
 Sited at the cross roads,
Country goods on market days
 Were sold there by loads.

Mainly, butter, eggs and such fare
 Were on sale at the cross,
Only fresh for a little while
 The stone gathered no moss.

Business was brisk on trading days
 No time to swan around,
Sell the goods, get paid up
 Then go homeward bound.

Back at the farm, sighs of relief
 Surplus goods had sold,
Round the kitchen fireside
 Diverse yarns were told –

Of bargains made and sales technique
 How to close a deal,
Fellow vendors all partook
 Of ale and a hearty meal.

The Plague Pit

In some village churchyards
    There is still to be found,
A plot with iron railings
    The plague pit to surround.

In mid seventeenth century
    Plague raged in the towns,
Too many to bury singly
    Dumped as one in ground.

Just thrown in altogether
    Peasant and lord the same,
A mixture of bloated bodies
    The plague chose to claim.

Few were the survivors
    Labour was needed badly,
They named their price to work
    Toiled in fields most gladly.

It was an ill fed wind
    That spread the germs so dire,
Leaving a trail of terror
    From manor house to byre.

Yet still the germs live on
    In the pit underground
No one must disturb the site
    That is iron-clad bound.

What If?

What if there had been no Adam
There would have been no Eve,
    There would be no Jesus Christ
In whom we can believe.

What if Julius Caesar
Had not invaded our shores,
    There would be no Hadrian's wall
Or Roman roads galore.

What if the holocaust
Had not taken place,
    Would Hitler's plan of action
Still be in disgrace.

If Jesus had not existed
There would be no ministry,
    No, miracles, no healing
No ordeal on Calvary.

What if I had been born a male
Would parents have been pleased,
    Instead I'm a querying female
In whom powers of reason are squeezed.

Tenacity

The ability to cling and carry on
With a cause that seems lost,
    You know it is right
Regardless of the cost.

A quest that must be pursued
With energy and strength,
    Must be worth the battle
However hard and intense.

The quality of tenacity
Belongs to a very few,
    Dedication in the fight
Shows an end result and true.

The desired effect of winning
Adversaries on the run,
    To be let down gently
Now that you have won.

Graciousness in victory
Will set you well apart,
    Proves your seeking for the truth
Reveals a courageous heart.

A Borg Cube

An ugly means of transport
    Black, fast and efficient,
Preying on the weak and trapped
    Menacing and malevolent.

A Borg cube is one of hoards
    That to the collective belong,
Assimilating knowledge
    To them is not wrong –

Merely to pursue perfection
    That's their ultimate goal,
Automaton, changed human
    Who's left without their soul.

Straight in the Star-trek pages
    We find the threat of Borg,
A terrifying, unwanted future
    Better to be in the morgue.

Then along comes man and Voyager
    With Janeway wading in,
Representing human determination
    Fighting the Borg, she wins.

Which only goes to show
    It pays to search for the way,
To defeat the formidable enemy
    Dig in heels, stand firm and pray.

Side by Side

few animals went in side by side
　　Enticed into the Ark,
Plant collections eggs and seeds
　　Saved as Noah embarked –

On a journey to preserve all life
　　From the rising waters,
Would food and water supplies
　　Feed his sons and daughters.

Until the waters had receded
　　And the Ark beached on land,
His captive population
　　Had started to expand.

Some beasts had produced their young
　　So he set a raven free,
To find dry land to disembark
　　But nothing was there to see.

Later he sent out a dove
　　To find land and explore,
It came back with a green leaf
　　Firm evidence of more.

They could now safely unload
　　Relieve the cramped conditions,
Plant the plants, sow the seeds
　　The end of their holy mission.

Why Mess Up Time?

Twice a year, we mess up time
 Change the Greenwich mean,
Disorientating many people
 It really is obscene.

Called daylight saving
 All it does is annoy,
If not broken why fix it
 A silly foolish ploy.

Let's keep life simple
 Leave the clocks on GMT,
We should refuse to obey
 This irritating decree –

That throws us in confusion
 'Til we don't know horse from cart,
Why don't they understand
 We much prefer the dark.

The Path of Destiny

Do we choose or just wander
Along the path of destiny,
Unknowing and confused
    As an illness, weak to see –

Underneath our thin veneer
There lurks the primitive soul,
That staggers along each route
    And painfully evolves.

A little culture or compassion
Has matured in the very few,
We must consider each path we take
    Or we may come to rue.

It may, by chance, be right
Were we pushed or guided,
The path of destiny leads us
    To lifestyles still divided –

By the way we treat each other
And abuse our planets beasts,
And pay too much attention
    To hypocritical priests.

Who wring their hands in glee
And preach indoctrination,
Telling us we should repent
    Or reap dire recrimination –

    Through their own interpretations.

The Sun Sinks Softly

As the sun sinks softly
    At close of its allotted day,
A human life is fading
Beneath the darkened ray.

At end of its permitted span
    This life's been full of hope,
Now the time has come
The spirit to elope.

The sun touches this bit of life
    With a gentle, soothing balm,
Ensuring that the passing over
Is achieved with all due calm.

There are no regrets at all
    Of the long, extended years,
Ambitions realised, and family ties
Mingled with hopes and fears.

Now as the sun sinks softly
    Daylight has to make way,
For comforting cape of night
Is anchored here to stay.

Faith

ꝼaith is guaranteed to get you through
Whatever life may throw,
Faith will sustain your resolve
    And show which way to go.

There is a basic need in man
For a faith to lay down rules,
A code of conduct for all mankind
    From wise men down to fools.

Faith in the soul's ability
To weather all the storms,
Inspiration that can be drawn
    From prophets in many forms –

Who trod the earth long ago,
Believed in the Hebrew God,
Were controlled by the priesthood's
    Iron laws, a strict ramrod.

Nevertheless, we all need faith
As much as food and water,
So we can traverse life's road
    With fellow sons and daughters.

Injuries

There are too many to list
Cannot make a start,
Damage can be sustained
　　To any body part.

Traffic accidents cause many
Or self inflicted stab,
Injury will occur to harm
　　When a sharp knife is had.

Great pain comes with injuries
Of all assorted kinds,
Damaging the body
　　And shattering the mind.

Broken limbs can be healed
Encased in a plaster cast,
The bone will knit in time
　　And plaster comes off fast.

There is one type of injury
That's restricted to one part,
The desertion of a loved one
　　Totally breaks the heart.

Good Friday

There is nothing good about this day
The world should learn to mourn,
The death of Christ the Lord
    Left by God all forlorn –

To die on Calvary's cross
Supposedly for us all,
It can only be a story
    Passed on in home and hall.

To some it was useful
A piece of propaganda,
Spread by priests to whom
    Our children have to pander.

Christ lived amongst humankind
Under Jewish/Roman rule,
He healed the sick, preached the word
    Showed he was nobody's fool.

He was a living example
Of how to live on earth,
Revered and followed to the end
    From the moment of his birth.

Easter Day

Easter day is Easter Sunday
A day of happiness and joy,
    Resurrection's celebration
Followed swiftly by Easter Monday.

'Tis said that on the third day
Christ left his dismal tomb,
    And appeared to his lady
The stone had just rolled away.

Full of doubts she went off to tell
The others all waiting there,
    He is risen was the cry
He is alive and well.

So the story thru' the years
Is told and retold again,
    Holiday break for Christian folk
However it may appear.

We are safe in the knowing
Christ was a real person,
    By following his way of life
Our belief will be showing.

He Rode On a Donkey

He rode on a humble donkey
Of strange, simple brown,
For his entry to Jerusalem
The major Jewish town.

Palms thrown in the road
Landed at his feet,
Where the donkey plodded
Cheers rang in the streets.

A portent of events to come
Jewish elders had planned,
To send him to his death
As a felon in the land.

Caring not for the Son of God
They harassed the little beast,
Until the crowd stopped their shouts
And joyous anthems were released.

Lackeys to the Caesar
They towed the Roman line,
Puzzled by no resistance
Their charges could not define.

Blameless, Christ stood before Pilate
Who could not him condemn,
The governor feared an uprising
From this trial would stem.

The rest is all history
Recorded down the ages,
The donkey rider died and lived
Again, says the Bibles' pages.

Out of Oblivion

$\mathcal{I}$nto this world knowing nothing
And later pushed away,
I viewed life with mainly
    Disappointment and dismay.

Discounted as a person
No rights to any views,
Into oblivion my psyche
    Was placed, lost amongst the truth.

I tried a way to improve my lot
The wasted years, hard work grafted,
To line a loved ones pockets
    Proved his love had not lasted.

I found the recipe to breath
On my own, out of oblivion,
I slowly crawled to seek the stars
    And learned the joys of living.

To express in poetic verse
My ideas, feelings, thought,
To reveal my deep belief
    Recognition can't be bought.

The Greatest Enemy

Time is the greatest enemy
Constantly stealing life,
Leaving just a hollow shell
Of what was once so blithe –

A person, full of verve and go
Who made a mark on time,
Producing deeds remarkable
Precious memories entwined.

Time has betrayed the body
Robbed, aged, struck down,
Mobility so reduced that
What's left is just a clown.

The greatest enemy of all
Lops off several years,
From our likely life span
Cutting short careers –

A contented way of life
For couples together wed,
Who with each other walk
Are hand in hand led.

Togetherness, the comforter
Foremost in older years,
Soothing problems when time
The greatest enemy appears.

June Roses

The warm sixth month of the year
When all the roses bloom
Fragrant, teas and ramblers wild
Delightfully revealed in June.

Roses, the favourite flower of all
Shatter and fade too soon,
Petals fall in park and garden
By day and light of moon.

Many, the beds of the lovely rose
Wherever they may be found,
The rose will grow, come what may
In any type of ground.

The emblem of England's pride
Regardless of its name,
The rose has endued the years
A symbol to be acclaimed.

Let the roses bloom again
Let English hearts in tune,
Beat as only English can
Constantly, not just in June.

The Conscience of the People

The conscience of the people
Is buried deep, down inside,
The philosophy of the poet
Serves to be our guide.

The conscience of the people
Should tell us what to do,
The philosophy of the poet
Will take us safely through.

What is right and what is wrong
Which course should we take?
Does the philosophy of the poet
In truth perhaps, indicate.

It is a moral responsibility
For the poet, to understand
To inform, guide the people
By the language of his hand.

Our leaders need to heed the voice
That dwells within the conscience
Of our nations people, oft
Spoken by the poet's inner sense.

Stranded

We had no idea of problems
    When in Spain we landed,
The volcanic ash cloud
    Ensured that we were stranded.

Mum tried hard to make contact
    But could only reach Mandy,
That was because she always
    Keeps her mobile handy.

Worried sick Mum was frantic
    Got into a panic state,
As one of our party
    Is in condition delicate.

Mum loves us all to bits
    She really starts to moan,
Flights should not have been cancelled
    We should be safely home.

A distressing situation
    Trying all sorts of routes,
Whilst Gordon's false government
    Doesn't give a hoot.

I Only Laugh

 I do not laugh when people trip
Or generally take a tumble,
I only laugh when a pompous ass
    Is forced to becoming humble.

I do not laugh at a funeral
Of family or a friend,
I only laugh when a despot
    Is driven round the bend.

I do not laugh at owner's devotion
To their beloved pet,
I only laugh when hecklers
    Cause politicians to sweat.

I do not laugh when people praise
A popular idol or star,
I only laugh, when it shows
    What shallow folk they are.

I do not laugh at monarchists
Who regard royalty with awe,
I only laugh, ask the question
    What are they really for?

I do not laugh at members
Ensconced within the House,
I only laugh when it's proved
    Most are just a louse.

Election 2010

It is another special year
　　　They've called an election,
Most of the populace
　　　Can't make wise selection.

People dither, and hesitate
　　　Supposedly to have choice,
But do their elected members
　　　Listen to their voice?

No, the promises are broken
　　　Life goes on as before,
The party that's in power
　　　Help themselves to more.

Policy is flaunted generally
　　　As being a matter of prime,
Why not put England first?
　　　Just once upon a time.

Our country needs strong leaders
　　　To get us out of mess,
Unpopular spending cuts, where?
　　　It's anybody's guess.

Vote for stability, vote for change
　　　They all drone on and on,
Shall be glad when it's over
　　　Whichever party's won?

The Holiday Month

The holiday month of July
Drags many families away,
Kids off school, bored to tears
Long for the holidays.

Seaside, beach, sea and sand
The grit gets everywhere,
Between our toes, in our shoes,
And even in our hair.

Sandwiches aptly named
Grate on gum and teeth,
Drying out swimming clothes
Finds sand underneath.

Caravan beds, hard and narrow
Condensation drips down walls,
Generally cramped conditions
Great time for one and all.

Hotel life fares better
More space and comfort,
Bargain breaks as advertised
Are most keenly sort.

Come the end of holiday time
Pack up and travel home,
It's good to be back here
Wherever we have roamed.

Christmas Carols

Christmas carols fill the air
With a melodious, full refrain,
    Reminding us it's about
Christ's birthday time again.

How many of us really believe
In the wonder of His birth?
    Lay down arms, hold a truce
Celebrate peace on earth.

The message of Christmas carols
Is to shelve those matters sad,
    It's a time of great rejoicing
Be of good cheer, laugh and be glad.

Let the carols ring out
In every home and hall,
    Not just for the church goers
But for everyone and all.

So, join in with the carols
Fully take a part,
    Let the Christmas carols
Sound within our hearts.

Why Has a Long Tail

Why do I get the urge to write
Am I afraid to fail?
No it is simply because
Why has a long tail.

Why is a chairman of a meeting
Changed to chair person,
It is political correctness
Gone too far in version.

Why does a street sign say
P Here, but if you do
You will have landed yourself
Knee deep in the poo.

What happened to the golliwog
Adorning marmalade jar?
That is just race relations
Carried away too far.

Why can't we be patriotic
And fly St George's cross,
After all we are English folk
Let's show who is boss.

Why do I go on writing verse
To keep from going stale?
The answer is abundantly clear
Why has a very long tail.

A Mixed Bouquet

I have tried in my poems
  To illustrate views of peace,
Hoping that in future years
  Killing wars will cease.

A varied bouquet of lines
  Written from feelings deep,
Trusting that posterity will
  My efforts safely keep.

I've touched on many subjects
  Nature coming to the fore,
Childhood dreams to reality
  Featured in the core.

Disappointments, failures, the like
  Have all been in my verse,
I wonder then, are we
  Heirs of an ancient curse.

No excuses will cover up
  A fundamental flaw,
That may lurk in the psyche
  Driving men to war.

In all my written work
  I have tried by assorted verse,
To form a marriage in a book
  Either better, or worse.

My Cousin Went to Oz

Steve left us all behind
When he emigrated there,
I recall the days when
    Fun and games we shared.

Outdoor meals and rambles vast
Around the farm we went,
Days of happy childhood
    School holidays were spent.

The gap he left is hard to define
When my cousin went to Oz,
I know I feel to this day
    A huge sense of loss.

I have not seen him many times
Since he left his native folk,
I trust one day I will again
    Listen to his jokes.

He had the knack of raising smiles
He was a dreadful tease,
Knowing when to make a jibe
    And knowing when to please.

I wish he would soon return
Just for a hug and a kiss,
Then I can tell him to his face
Keith has worked such wonders
    Our team work can be bliss.

It's a Hot Summers Day

It's a hot summers day
Defying attempts to keep cool,
The fan does a great job
　　A very useful tool.

Moving air round the room
Causing a welcomed draught,
Laying out in the sun
　　Is sheer folly and daft.

Why try to get brown skin
Who wants to be tanned?
It is harmful to the skin
　　Really should be banned.

These cancers are all caused
By exposure to the sun,
For those of fair colouring
　　Definitely not fun.

Fair people greatly suffer
In the sun's burning rays,
Better in the shade, and
　　Hope for temperate days.

There is no merit in turning brown
Receiving a nasty sunburn,
With half an hour exposure
　　You'll be done to a turn.

Odd One Out

I was the odd one out
Not the proud and haughty kind,
But shy, timid, reticent
　　Who was always left behind.

I was often the odd one out
Embarking on my quest,
Rebelling against rules laid down
　　By those said to know best.

I questioned their set opinions
Queried the lack of reason,
The narrow-minded hard-line
　　That dominated every season.

Being the odd one out
Made me feel afraid,
Of the perils of life itself
　　And pitfalls that were laid.

Yet it was from odd ones out
That our greatest leaders came,
Nelson, Churchill and the ilk
　　All ones that rose to fame.

Not pretending to be great
Nor deemed myself as wise,
I persisted in my pilgrimage
　　And learnt the hows and whys.

It's Bank Holiday Monday

It's Bank Holiday Monday,
The final day of May,
The weather's grim and dull
    One more cold, windy day.

Why is it always so?
When banks are not open,
The weather surely turns sour
    Are we fondly hoping –

For a last minute change
With warmth and sunlight,
To cheer us up once more
    Making the day all right.

It's rare for a good day
When crowds flock to the sea.
Now they find cold and damp
    Adding to their misery.

Traffic jams hog the roads
And tempers begin to fray,
Shrug the shoulders, carry on
    Just another Bank Holiday.

The Human Race

Where do we think we're going
Where is the starting place?
Is it a strange competition
    Or simply the human race?

We strive throughout our short lives
To be first passed the post
What is the purpose
    To get ahead of most?

Is it really a tough contest
Do we really have to enter?
Life is so difficult
    Aim straight for the centre.

To rush about and thrash around
Is not the best of ways,
Relaxing and love of nature
    Ensures much happier days.

Engineered by ancient gods
To dig and delve underground,
To mine for them precious gold
    That for Niburu was bound.

Earth was stripped of needed metals
Taken to the shipping place,
Off to their distant planet
    Thanks to the human race.

Part of man's great struggle
Cloaked by a subtle disguise,
To constantly achieve
    And guarantee first prize.

Back to School

'Though it is only August
Holidays are almost over,
Preparations are being made
   From Scotland down to Dover.

Books and pencils are now ready
Bags, lunch boxes too,
Many little children are
   Starting something new.

In through the iron gates
Some feeling rather glum,
Different ways to pass the day
   End of time with Mum.

Parking is always a problem
Near and next the school,
Some parents park unwisely
   Many ignore the rules.

Blocking up the roads
Impeding traffic flow,
Motorists loudly curse
   Wanting them to go.

It is dangerous to park
Both sides of a village street,
Just a little further off
   This problem they would defeat.

Romantic at Heart

$\mathcal{B}$eing basically romantic
 I only see the best,
Ignoring the greater whole
 That makes up the rest.

The greater part not on show
 A dark side of a being,
I stumble on a fatal course
 Refusing to be seeing –

The harm coming hand in hand
 To a romantic heart,
Stupid, foolish viewpoint
 Doomed right from the start.

There is so little goodness
 In mans very nature,
There is inherent badness
 A non-romantic feature.

Reality is hard to comprehend
 For the romantic heart,
The dream is just fantasy
 Horse behind the cart –

Yet, there is someone out there
 So take a different path
You will find a soul-mate
 And a love that will last.

Death of Paper

Will we really see the death of paper?
In this fast electronic age,
Authors will be quite put off
    Without the printed page.

It will be so sad to see
All their work confined to disc,
The beautiful bound volumes
    Will be so sorely missed.

What will be the point of writing?
If there are no printed books,
The compacted version defies
    Any attempted good looks.

Yet, in some well-kept library
Will be found the printed tomes,
Preserved in this treasure trove
    Revered, their last and only home.

So authors do not give up
Write without sign of despair,
Your work is for the benefit
    Of whoever visits there.

Law and Order

It is the solemn duty
For units of law and order,
To protect the populace
    And defend our borders.

What do they do instead?
They enforce the law with a twist,
Choosing to prosecute instead
    The vulnerable motorist.

Immigrants pour into our country
Unhindered by the law,
We are bursting at the seams
    There is no room for more.

The welfare state, open to abuse
Pays out, illegal claims,
Panders to human rights
    Whilst the law is seen as lame.

Law and order should protect
The citizens of this land,
Giving a sense of security
    Our guardians close at hand.

Summertime in August

August, a dignified imposing stance
The hottest month of the year,
Long hours of daylight increase
Demands for cold, iced beer.

Augustus, the Roman Caesar
Ordered the census of Jews,
At time of birth of Christ
For Caesar not good news.

As it's usually hot in August
Sleeping not easy at night,
Too hot, stuffy by far
Perspiring is our plight.

We have learned to rely
On fans to move the air,
Cooling currents in bedrooms
Assist our sleeping there.

So August comes in midsummer
When the land is bone dry,
How we long for rain clouds
To gather in the sky.

Second Best

When I loved I truly loved
    With my body, heart and soul,
To give you peace and prosperity
    That was my only goal.

I loved you more than life itself
    Far more than I could say,
I wish you loved me the same
    With no obstacles in the way.

No matter what I did or said
    I felt it was not enough,
I worked hard every day
    And found the going tough.

But that is how it was
    I suffered deep unrest,
I wondered why in your heart
    I always came second best.

I had a massive chip
    Ugly on my shoulder,
Yet, I dumped the hurt at last
    As I grew wiser and older.

Early Morning Light

It was very early morning
Without a glimmer of light,
Horizon was still quite dark
    Just as the dead of night.

Yet, from a bush outside
Came a twitter of waking birds,
The dawn chorus commenced
    They barely could be heard.

A finger of orange lit the sky
The suns single ray,
Heralded, a promise to all
    A splendid summer's day.

Louder and louder grew bird's song
Pheasant, blackbird and thrush,
In the hunt for morning snacks
    Welcomed the early blush –

That lit the sky with radiant hues
Enchanting with no compare,
Monarch of the east leading to
    Daylight warmth everywhere.

Now the sun is westward sinking
Crimson showing is the ray,
The moon adds her gentle light
    To aid the dying day.

Stalking

Creeping on its belly
Domestic cat stalks its prey,
But when it makes its catch
It only wants to play.

What feral, primeval instinct
Has spawned this ancient stalk,
A surer method of hunting
Than a conventional walk.

Lionesses of a scattered pride
Stalk gazelle and wildebeest,
A kill, made swiftly, ensures
Their cubs will have a feast.

They seem to enjoy the hunt
Scenting, food along the track,
Springing out suddenly
Upon the victim's back –

For the alpha male has first pick
Of the females prize,
He tears away satisfactorily
Surveying all his wives.

The human kind of stalker
Is quite a different kind,
Bringer of worry and uncertainty
He preys upon the mind.

Hopefully, his reign is short
He will soon be caught
A term behind prison bars
Will end his idea of sport.

The Pheasant

A pheasant landed in the garden
Took shelter in the shade,
    Shuffled her heated body
Into a hole she made.

Hot and tired from incubation
She needed a welcomed break,
    She longed for some rainfall
Her raging thirst to slake.

Wallowing in the hole
Getting dust in her feathers,
    Sending a few irate fleas
Scurrying off in a dither.

After squirming in the dust
She remembered her quest,
    The cock-bird still on guard
Not far from the nest.

Over the fence into the field
She landed in the grass,
    Back on the nest again
Resuming her domestic task.

Soon the eggs would hatch
Little chicks scarcely seen,
    Running in the verdant meadow
Amongst the protective green.

The Horseman of the Woods

In the deepest part of the wood
A headless horseman rides,
The sight of him so fearful
      That everybody hides.

When the moon is high and full
There can oft be heard the sound,
Of horses hooves in the wood
      Hammering on the ground.

Sometimes a very brave soul
Would dare to stay in sight,
In case the headless horseman
      Should ride again that night.

How did this apparition
Come to be in this state?
It was due to the betrayal
      By the horseman's mate.

She showed the sheriff's men
Where he lay in bed,
In the ensuing fight
      Her lover lost his head.

The lady was in anguish
Being full of remorse,
She cleared the way, for his ghost
      To ride again his horse.

Birthday Tribute

It is the twenty eighth of June
Birthday of my son,
The biggest of the three
    A gentle giant of fun.

Foremost a family man
With boy and girl he adores,
Growing up so very fast
    Is there room for more?

Of the three brothers
So far the only one,
That's managed to provide
    This generations son.

I, the proud mother of these boys
Pay tribute to what's been done,
I say with all my heart
    Happy birthday, eldest son.

Mellow September

The warm, mellow month of September
When grain matures to harvest,
Ripe apples, pears and other fruits
　　Are ravished by many pests.

Wasps, beetles, earwigs, the lot
Chew away inside the shell,
Turning tempting, juicy fruit
　　To a messy, rotten smell.

Nature knows no pity
When harvest comes too quick,
Early dry months ensures
　　Sparse produce there to pick.

If the growing season
Suffers from lack of rain,
Plants have little moisture
　　To swell the ripening grain.

Conversely in a good year
The harvest grows with zest,
Plentiful produce ripened well
　　We enjoy the very best.

In spite of mans technology
And sophisticated tools,
In mellow September and every month
　　Mother Nature rules.

Hard Cheese

Not a delicacy to eat
But just designed to tease,
An expression of indifference
　　　To put as Hard Cheese.

So what, another way to say
And not intended to please,
Really do not care at all
　　　It's tough this Hard Cheese.

Like a British Rail sandwich
Dried up bread and cheese,
Disgusting, offending food
　　　Straight out of the freeze.

Improperly wrapped to consume
Balanced on eater's knees,
What is needed is fresh fare
　　　No more tasteless Hard Cheese.

Sandwiches in the buffet car
Could really tempt the buyer,
If travellers found them new
　　　Unlike a rubber tyre.

Why is the cost of commuter food
Sky high as legal fees?
It is the attitude adopted
　　　So what, that's Hard Cheese.

The Shell

The tide reached the shell
    Half buried in the sand,
Once the beach was high and dry
All part of fertile land.

The shell was kissed with salt water
    Whirling round the dirt,
Filling out the crevices
With each welcomed squirt.

How long had the shell lain there?
    What tales could it tell?
Of drowning ship-wrecked sailors
Submerged just where they fell.

The shell longed to be at sea
    Not stranded on the shore,
It wanted to hear the pounding waves
And be alive once more.

Once it contained a body
    A soft vulnerable oyster,
Now dried out on the beach
Entirely without moisture.

As the tide turned back to ebb
    The shell was pulled to sea,
Right out of the gripping sand
Bringing the shell its liberty.

Chip off the Old Block

There was once a young woodsman
Of ancient yeoman stock,
Like his father long before him
    A chip off the old block.

He tended the forest trees
Cutting with great care,
Aware of a maiden's gaze
    Intense, lustful stare.

Bashful, shy to the 'nth degree
He wished she would say,
Why she hid in the woods
    To watch him every day.

He loved truly her from afar
In her country lass's frock,
He showed his rippling muscles
    A chip off the old block.

His father had taken a lass
From the house of feudal lord,
He overstepped the mark
    And was killed by a sword.

The son felt the rising sap
His heart wide open to mock,
The lady wanted him to be
    A chip off the old block.

February Love

It's fourteenth of February again
The time of Valentine,
　　When declarations of love
Are poetically made in rhyme.

To tell the heart's desire
Of their forever love,
　　Optimistic statements cooed
By billing turtledoves.

Images of hearts co-joined
Pieced by Cupids arrow,
　　Time will soon reveal
A love-life so narrow –

That cannot stay the course
Another love will interlope,
　　The forever love illusion
Is another forlorn hope.

It would be wonderful
If forever, love could be kept,
　　No more painful heartache
Or tears to be wept.

Sport of Kings

Galloping fast on the straight
As though the beast had wings,
Over heath, field and meadow
    Racing, the sport of kings.

Lots of punters wage their bets
On which horse will win,
Too many will lose their shirt
    And bear it with a grin –

But others can ill afford to lose
Bet money not their own,
Hanging heads, ashamed they crawl
    Very slowly to their homes.

They have squandered house keeping
Saved to purchase food,
The lady of the stricken house
    Is in an ugly mood.

Many times it has occurred
No sense or restraint applied,
Will they ever learn?
    Get off the slippery slide.

Only those who can afford
The loss should have a fling,
Emulating HRH in
    Applauding their sport of kings.

The Aircraft

The aircraft limped across the sky
    Visibility being just a haze,
Crew tried to scramble free
It was well ablaze.

Shot up by enemy fighter
    Not much hope was there,
Time was fast running out
For Lancaster in the air.

Far from home landing field
    Out of fuel supply,
Lost its altitude now, and
Plummeted from the sky.

Straight into the ground below
    Killing all the crew,
Heroes of Britain's struggle
Valiant, through and through.

Who bought us breathing space
    From raving Hitler's fury,
These boys, too young to die
Covered themselves in glory.

Janus

Janus, the Roman god
Who managed to look two ways,
One side facing to the east
    The other a westerly gaze.

Both sides of the same coin
Rivals for great esteem,
Reality, harsh for one
    Other side, hopeful dream.

One face, the old year fades
Flip side, the new year comes,
All part of the calendar
    Two sides, instead of one.

Presented as god of deceit
Janus saw two ways,
Preferring to hedge his bets
    Caring not who pays.

In life, it is impossible
To sit on the fence,
Decisions must be taken
    In spite of the consequence.

Shame

They hang their heads in shame
    Having been caught out,
Telling lies, doing evil deeds
That's what it is about.

Stealing another's property
    All part of the shame,
Felt by the perpetrator
Who has to take the blame.

Causing deliberate harm
    To another living person,
Makes him wonder why
No one believes his version.

In some eastern countries
    Punishment is not bland,
Theft results in the robber
Losing one of his hands.

Brits are of the opinion
    That action's too severe,
Just tap them on the wrist
Is the judgement over here.

There is very little shame today
    No matter what the crime,
No one gives a stuff about
The mess that's left behind.

Destiny

$\mathfrak{S}$ome people fail all their lives
Were born to look a fool,
Trying hard to gain success
    Just another's tool.

Strong persons exploit weakness
Usually for personal gain,
The lesser one will always strive
    Their favour to obtain.

Why is it that destiny
Leads so many diverse ways?
The path of life twists and turns
    Swamping losers in its maze.

There is a time to be strong
And time for gentleness,
Compassion brings much reward
    The holder is greatly blessed.

The most valued treasures are
Laughter, glee and mirth.
'Tis said the meek shall inherit
    These bounties of the earth.

Inspired

What mystic hand of old
Inspired those humble scribes
    To copy down such marvels
Before the tears had dried.

They needed faith and integrity
To keep at bay their fears,
    Facing execution and
Betrayal by their peers.

Heresy was a major crime
Learning possessed by few,
    Still they maintained their course
Remembering Jesus the Jew.

Banned by the law and order
In those persecuted days,
    They wrote down all they could
About Jesus and his ways.

Some versions came out altered
To others telling the story,
    All recorded by simple facts
Forever, placed in history.

Disciples, inspired to pen
Events of the Saviours life,
    They left open the question,
Whether he had a wife?

'Tis said Jesus lived for much longer
Than the Bible states,
    Will the end of days see
The return we all await?

The Door

When a tremendous row takes place
  Heated, nasty words will flow,
Slamming the door firmly shut
Leaves nowhere else to go.

What is it all about
  Why, you, you and just you?
It should occur in your mind that
There is another point of view.

Not listening to explanations
  Refusing to cede a jot,
Stalemate hanging in the air
Compromising not –

Gets both parties fixed
  Into a stupid jam,
Listening to the other one
Will surely break the damn.

Try hard to see reason
  With benefit of the doubt
Leaving the door just open
Provides a certain way out.

The moral of these lines
  Is to always compromise,
The other party may not
Be telling any lies.

A Touch of Insanity

You could hear her in the garden
    Using the foulest profanity,
All neighbours recognised
A touch of insanity.

Once a teacher in the school
    Until she became obsessed,
Hating all around her
Thoroughly depressed.

Unlike her genteel mother
    She was ex ATS,
Now swearing like a trooper
Her life now just a mess.

Tearing up the garden weeds
    As if they were humanity,
Frustrated to her very core
A touch of insanity.

She would feed her neighbours cats
    Causing many a calamity,
Blundering in the traffic
A sure sign of insanity.

Little Green Men from Mars

Are they from another dimension
    Or from realms beyond the stars?
Just visitors to our planet
These little green men from Mars.

Do they have a language
    Or simply rely on sign?
What are their intentions
Malignant or benign?

Reports are very rare
    Of them being seen,
So, how do we really know
That they are green?

Are we experiments in a lab
    Just rats in their maze,
Simple man on this earth
Is so easily fazed.

Have they guarded our intentions
    And guided us from the start,
Will they try to stop us
From blowing ourselves apart?

Do they marry or interbreed
    Feel pain, experience love?
Are their actions orchestrated
By a Grand Master from above.

Milking Time

The cows line up expectantly
For it is getting late,
Waiting for the farmer
    To open up the gate.

Once the gate is opened
They quicken their pace
Each has in the cowshed
    An individual place.

When the milking is over
They will all be fed,
Hay and mangel wurzels
    Portioned for each head.

Where is the inner clock
Telling it is milking time?
Sending to the yard gate
    And getting them in line.

Grazing in fields all day
Aided by the sun,
They know when it is time
    For milking to be done.

They wait patiently in place
For the farmer of the land,
To ease the heavy udder load
    With his warm, gentle hands.

Losing the Plot

There comes a point in life
When we loose the plot,
Mixing days of the week
    Confusing kettle with pot.

Is it breakfast or dinner
For some cannot tell,
Which is right or left
    Trapped in senile hell.

Why did you go upstairs
What was wanted there?
Forgetfulness displayed
    In need of loving care.

Memory plays rotten tricks
On the senior mind,
Events of long ago
    Become easier to find.

When short term memory quits
Takes a well earned break,
Long term is excellent and
    Never makes a mistake.

A penalty of getting old
Seemingly to loose the plot,
But does it really matter now
    When time is all you've got.

Death Intervenes

New baby born grows to infant
Child, man and stages between,
A lifespan, long could continue
    Except that death intervenes.

Childless monarchs long for heirs
Often blaming their queens,
Plans, new ideas still forming
    Until their death intervenes.

The executioner aims his blade
To fall swiftly and clean,
The victim does not suffer long
    As death soon intervenes.

Romantic lovers tie the knot
Over the anvil at Gretna Green,
Pledging to forsake all others
    Until death does intervene.

James Watt, the inventor
Saw the power of steam,
Was able to apply his talents
    Before his death intervened.

Lingering in a sick bed
Patients only able to scream,
Longing for the blessed release
    When death shall intervene.

Where Were You?

When the world was young
And little was about,
Were you in the queue
   When brains were handed out?

Few of us have talent
Most of us mundane,
Perhaps to re join the queue
   Should be our foremost claim.

Why are there so many
Who classify as dolts?
Were they last in the queue
   Was it really their fault?

Given another chance
Would we be just the same?
Or would there be displayed
   A fairer share of brain?

Alas 'tis not possible
To change our intellect,
The limited thinking of others
   We are compelled to accept.

In the hand-out department
Of the brain-box queue,
There remains one question
   Just where were you?

Valentine 2011 (I)

It is my duty to write
    A Valentine each year,
To express once again
How much I hold you dear.

There cannot be said too much
    How strong is our bond,
My love is brimming over
So good that you respond.

Our lives entwine like ivy
    Growing up the garden wall,
Where high up in the greenery
Our love shines through it all.

There are no obstacles
    We cannot overcome,
We will pull together
Til every battle is won.

We have so much in common
    Writing down our views,
Designing and editing
Leaves no time for the blues.

A legacy for the future
    Generations to come,
They can have the benefit
Once our work is done.

On the Move?

What restless spirit
Urges us to make a move?
When our current situation
    Will be hard to improve.

We have a pleasant cosy house
Roomy, with gardens fine,
Cannot take them with us
    Pity to leave behind.

The animals are safe here
Far enough from highway,
They can roam at leisure
    Investigate prowl and play.

We have collected furniture
Chosen pieces placed with flair,
It is only right, they
    Should remain in situ there.

There is room for both our cars
And also several more,
We have all we want
    Move, whatever for?

By George

By George an ancient battle-cry
    Of hostilities intended,
Only by fighting fierce
Can the bloody war be ended.

St George, not an English knight
    Just a common German soldier,
By his slaying of the dragon huge
He became the title holder.

Cry St George for England
    Shout it from shore to shore,
Our stalwart patron saint
Is needed now even more.

Once England had an empire
    Ruled wisely, extremely fair,
But just remnants are still left
No wonder we despair.

As part of the European Union
    We are tied by political cords,
This control freak must be severed
By George and freedoms sword.

The Stupid and the Brave

Flying in the face of danger
    Seeming to take a stand,
Puts other folk in danger
What lives are in their hands.

Our brave wartime pilots
    Went up and up again,
Regardless of the terror
And losses of their planes.

They flew against superior odds
    Mustered by the Hun,
Thanks to their great courage
The Battle of Britain was won.

By contrast, overpaid youths
    Flout all the safety rules,
Driving with drink and drugs
Just ignorant, stupid fools.

Brave firemen fight the blaze
    Putting themselves at risk,
Sometimes their death results and
Then they are sorely missed.

Why do some idiots endeavour
    To carry knives and guns,
It's not so very clever
To die when you are young.

Opera?

The snobs idea of a musical?
Patronised by queens and kings,
Noise from a screeching soprano
Can painful earache bring.

The melodic tenor's voice
Teaches us all how to sing,
Enchanting, entrancing harmony
That in the theatre rings.

Notes delivered with feeling
From the lowest to the high,
Singers pour their hearts out
In Madame Butterfly.

The lure of Spanish bullfights
Is animated by De Bizet,
Supposed to be an art-form
Killing the bull at bay.

Even so, most operatic singing
Complimented by orchestra,
Sees lots of the vocalists
Rise to be a star.

A rich, full, magic refrain
Brings hot tears to the eyes,
A lump to the throat so
We are totally mesmerised.

Adverts

So much of my viewing time
Is taken up by adverts,
Spoiling my enjoyment
    Interruptions that divert –

Away from the programme
And ruin my pleasure,
They take far too long
    Marring my leisure.

Is it really necessary
To put on the guff?
So frequently I resort
    To turning them off.

I pay my TV licence
In order to enjoy,
Not to have the programme
    By idiots destroyed.

Brash young women toss their heads
Patronisingly vane,
I will never buy the products
    'Cos it's money down the drain.

The same women prance about
In tatty clothes, so rough,
Why don't the advertisers twig
    I've really had enough?

When the Chips Are Down

If the chips are down
 Have things gone sadly wrong,
Has life lost its meaning
 The heart lost its song?

The bills come pouring in
 Mounting up quite gaily,
What should be done now as
 The debt increases daily?

When the chips are down
 Which is the way to go?
A knight champion is needed
 To set your face aglow.

To guide your course and put you
 In charge of the situation,
Cutting the spending spree
 Is the way to salvation.

Having done that and won reprieve
 Daylight gleams ahead,
Do not repeat the errors
 That filled your life with dread.

Life has so much to offer
 Even when chips are down,
You can find the happiness
 To take away the frown.

Golden October

Ripe October, the golden month
   Carries the year into autumn,
The leaves have all turned gold
The daylight hours will shorten.

Night time will then extend
   With evenings growing cold,
Harvest produce garnered
Marketed and sold.

At the end of October
   Falls ghostly Halloween,
When goblins, scary witches
Intrude upon the scene.

The warm colours of autumn
   Russet, red and gold,
Fond memories of summer
In these colours we behold.

Golden October rolls around
   Each year appreciated,
If the short autumn days
To contentment are related.

The Struggle

Sometimes I struggle with a poem
Just cannot get it right,
It is as if I'm infected
    With a deadly kind of blight.

The words will not flow at all
Appear stuck in my head,
It takes simply ages
    To get it put to bed.

A mental block takes charge
Crippling my creation,
I have to relax a bit
    To remedy the situation.

Life is a constant struggle
Against one foe or another,
Sometimes in conflict, it seems
    To be hardly worth the bother.

At last, in time I'm getting there
My ideas are finally sorted,
I had to struggle hard and
    Many attempts were aborted.

So is it worth a struggle
In order to get things right?
In every walk of life
    Daybreak still follows night.

Glorious Twelfth?

Creeping about on the grouse-moors
Now it is the shooting season,
A killing spree, blood sport
Lacking in rhyme and reason.

Charging round, firing guns
Boasting and showing off,
Strutting through purple heather
Just to mingle with the toffs.

Grouse, not needed for food
Are slaughtered en-masse,
Wounded birds limp away
Bleeding in the grass.

It is wrong to kill like this
So many of natures own,
They have a right to live
And should be left alone.

The moors a place of beauty
Fresh, clean air promoting health,
But not for the poor red grouse
Who die on the glorious twelfth.

November Mists

Rolling down from the hills
Drifting softly in the dales,
November's mists cloak the land
    In a murky, foggy veil.

Muting noise into silence
With obscured visibility,
Lorries and cars just crawl along
    As they cannot see.

Major road signs flash urgently
Warning drivers of the haze,
November mists have descended
    Blanketing the motorways.

November, end of autumn
Grips us in winter's fang,
On the fitth bonfires blaze
    Fireworks add their bang.

November's mists float away
As sun pierces the gloom,
A few daylight hours left
    Ere the fog entombs.

The Other Woman

The other woman is always there
    In spite husband saying no,
She breaks up home and family
She is the deadliest foe.

She has no good conscience
    She just does not care,
The pain and hurt she brings
Driving some wives to despair.

Husband chose to play away
    Spurning his faithful wife,
He grabbed everything he could
To make another life.

The other woman a predator
    Leeching what's not hers,
Aspiring to take another's spouse
She will be forever cursed.

The spurned wife struggles on
    Left empty and un-repleted,
The other woman should beware
Things can get overheated.

The other woman should back off
    Preserving the status quo,
She should quit the scene
Whilst she is able to go.

Welcome to Our World

Welcome to the world little one
Joining my expanding family,
You will be loved and admired
By doting Mum and proud Daddy.

As a grandmother many times
You are my latest star,
Lighting our lives each day, as
Angels guard wherever you are.

Late in time, as was our Lord
A big newcomer to me,
Greetings young lad, grandson
Welcome our baby Finley.

Your parents stand so very proud
You are their first boy,
Grow and thrive in their care
A bundle of love and joy.

The Greatest Enemy

Man's greatest enemy has
Committed the greatest crime,
Short'ning our span on earth
　　This old enemy, called time.

We should live a lot longer
Enjoying much better health,
The greatest enemy has
　　Stolen all by stealth.

We spend so little time
In the best part of life,
Time comes along and
　　Terminates like a knife.

Away from home and family
From loved ones we hold dear,
We have no way of knowing
　　When the end is near.

There is no sense in brooding
One cannot hope to defeat,
Time defies all known logic
　　There is no way to cheat.

Time, master of our destiny
By accident or plan,
We must question the status quo
　　To bring longevity to man.

The Wee Small Hours

The wee small hours of solitude
Panics the restless brain,
Demons of the night emerge
    Bringing both fear and pain.

Fear of the great unknown
Of evil that lurks within,
Tiredness confusing the mind
    Can't tell right from sin.

The brain, over-active
Panicking, full of cares,
Tries to cope with fright,
    As dreams turns to nightmares.

Must get out, get away
Is the message we receive,
Too many obstacles stand
    Blocking the way to leave.

The wee small hours of morning
Are they designed to scare?
Or, is it we should resort
    To a sane and simple prayer?

End of the World

It's been predicted many times
Foretold from long ago,
When the time finally comes
    Rivers of blood will flow.

Doom and gloom, hand in hand
Wiping out the human race,
Is it all in retribution
    Due to our fall from grace?

We rebelled against the ancient gods
Refused to work as slaves,
Bombardment from the skies above
    Will send millions to their graves.

The end of the world is nigh
It's been said many times,
But, always after catastrophe
    A few have been left behind.

It is surely going to happen
As the bible story says,
The mighty one in charge
    Will order the end of days.

He had tried before to destroy
By means of deluging rain,
Promised a few that survived, he
    Will not try that again.

Will We Meet Again?

This question has been asked
Throughout all the ages,
Reflected in the ponderings
　　Of histories sages.

There are some who believe
We to higher plane ascend,
That all our transgressions will
　　Automatically mend.

Some others who mock this view
Do not have the needed vision,
To see what is obviously
　　The prophets of old mission.

So the question will still be asked
And queries will remain,
Loved ones, gone on before
　　Will we meet again?

Simply put, the human spirit
Transcends all aspects vain,
Triumphantly it rises high
　　'Til we meet again.

Just Five Years

It is now five years
Since we decided to tie the knot,
Ending the time of punishment
    For crimes we knew not.

We had been there before
Marriage and what it was about?
Nevertheless, we were filled
    With thoughts of varied doubt.

Would friends and family
Come enjoy a look?
Or would they cause a row
    Before we signed the book?

On the day all went well
Good time had by all,
Guests mingled happily
    No sign of a brawl.

No regrets for the past five years
It's been for us so right,
We swapped a time of darkness
    For days of joyful light.

Marriage, a mixed bargain for two
Understanding all the quirks,
Solid love will demonstrate
    That effort makes it work.

The Bore

It is the worse judgement
Anyone can have passed
On their contributions to
 The present, future and past.

It is hard to understand
How some folks ramble on,
Never getting to the crux
 Until the point has gone.

Or keep repeating
Over and over again,
Same silly words driving
 Their listeners quite insane.

Why doesn't someone say
"For goodness sake stop,
We've all heard enough
 You really are a flop."

If there is a point to be made
Then say it quite concisely,
Sticking to the facts puts
 The impact more precisely.

Never let it be said
This comment applies to you,
A boring person finds his
 Contemporaries in the queue.

Brief Carefree Time

There was a brief time long ago
　　When I was young and free,
No worries to drag me down
　　A good home and family.

Came the time, few years later
　　When everything went strange,
Robbed of all I loved, I found
　　My life completely changed.

Years further on, I met one man
　　A new home now we share,
He turned my life around
　　Showing great love and care.

Together we have trod life's path
　　Happily we write poetic verse,
I love this man to bits
　　He has removed the curse –

I felt I had been jinxed
　　My life not carefree,
With my husband, now I see
　　It all was meant to be.

The Elusive Unicorn

What magic powers does it possess?
This white, mystical unicorn,
Cure all ills, cast out evil
By strength of a single horn.

A graceful, elegant kind of horse
With hind legs of antelope,
Tail of lion, beard of goat
Symbol of eternal hope.

Some are known to have wings
And fly straight through the clouds,
Weaving in and out the mists
An awesome steed so proud.

The healing horn of unicorn
Very hard to locate,
This animal, unlike others, is
Never served on a plate.

To catch such a myth is
Many a sick persons dream,
Of all the mythical beasts
The unicorn reigns supreme.

To be healed and well again
By the magic, tricoloured horn,
Fit and young, cured of ills
Thanks to the elusive unicorn.

Superglue

There is no power on earth
That can come 'twixt me and you,
I will not be shaken off
    I'll stick like superglue.

I have the most surprising
Super-sticking capacity,
You will be amazed
    The strength of my tenacity.

I will not let you leave
No matter what the rift,
I'll stick by you always
    I will never shift.

What else can I say?
Every word is true,
I will forever be
    Your tube of superglue.

As we progress thru the years
Enjoying our time and leisure,
Come what may, I will stick
    To you my dearest treasure.

Giants on the Earth

There were giants on the earth
So the ancient scribes have told,
Results of interbreeding produced
    The mighty men of old.

The revered gods of Niburu
Saw the females here as fair,
Mated, so the offspring had
    A hybrid gene-pool shared.

Huge in stature and strong
Dwarfing their human brothers,
These demi-gods soon displayed
    Brute ignorance of their mothers.

Large in body and aggressive
They fought their own kind,
Wiping themselves out
    'Til none were left behind.

The warring gene implanted
By the lofty beings,
Destroyed the very species
    Created by their genius.

Simple, untouched man on earth
Feared these giants of old,
Who lived off humankind
    Ruthlessly and cold.

Some modified men survived
More by luck than brains,
The warlike inherited gene
    Regrettably remains.

December's Claim

The unique month of the year
December of Christian fame,
Christmas time, fades out the year
    In a calculated endgame.

The year has progressed through
Months of similar name,
Mostly dreary, wet and cold
    We constantly complain.

As it is the final month
Before we reach another verge,
On the edge of a new year
    Can the old and new merge?

What difference can it make
This special December claim?
When all join together
    At Christmas time again.

Hunting parties charge round
Old hound packs of fame,
For the poor hunted animal
    It's certainly end game.

This constant tradition
Is Christmas just a name?
To an end and a beginning
    Is it pagan just the same!

Last Gateway

*L*ife is a series of gateways
　　For all that dwell on earth
Gateways to be passed through
From the day of our birth.

Childhood stages are gates
　　As is learning to walk
More importantly, communicate
We learn how to talk.

Some gateways appear unclear
　　Whether an in or an out
Very few can hope to discover
What life's all about.

Many gateways are difficult,
　　Hard to negotiate,
Not giving up grants access
Before it is too late.

As old age approaches
　　Life goes off course and astray.
Thus the Reaper appears, to assist
Us through this last gateway.

Thinking of You

I often sit and ponder
Muse over life's little traps,
Set for the unwary and
    Open to stupid prats.

I wonder how it is that we
Arrived at this point in time,
As we have learned a little
    Of the master-race sublime.

We know things others deny
Things we know are not true,
So, I sit quietly and muse
    By thinking just of you.

You are my inspiration
You help my creativity.
Like you I gain pleasure
    From the pen's activity.

Thoughts rush round my head
Like a clumsy circus clown,
I wish I could halt the pace
    And slow the thinking down.

I would like to be seen
As a person with common sense,
I think of you and know I've
    Cast off life's pretence.

We Have Met Before

I know we've met before
In the dim and distant past,
The journey of our lives
    Is thus co-joined to last.

I just cannot remember
When in which remote place,
Two souls found happiness and
    Defied the boundaries of space.

We were meant to live and love
Throughout all the ages,
Soul-mates, bonding on the way
    Players on many stages.

Will we ever remember
Where it was we met?
When we first kissed each other
    Caught in kismet's net.

The illusion of freedom
When it was meant to be,
A part of the master-plan
    That controls our destiny.

We won't give up the task
Of trying to recall the time?
When our spirits first found solace
    And our hearts entwined.

Rolling in the Aisles

It is a comedian's job
To raise laughter and smiles,
If he's really good he will
    Have them rolling in the aisles.

The bringing forth of merriment
Fills our remotest parts,
With chuckling, enjoyment
    That tickles every heart.

To laugh in a crowd or alone
Can only be good for you,
Rib-tickling humour finds
    Escape from the blues.

A comedian is an artist
Whatever form his style,
He's only satisfied, when
    They are rolling in the aisles.

He always has a straight guy
Who cops the custard pies,
How the kids roll about when
    Mr Comic gets one in the eye.

Genuine comedians lift our lives
With talent standing out a mile,
Smut free jokes will keep us
    Rolling in the aisles.

Hibernation

Some animals have acquired the habit
Of entering a torpid state,
  Sleeping through the winter months
  They've learned to hibernate.

The dozy hedgehog crawls
Into a pile of autumn leaves,
  He knows he won't be disturbed
  By the strong winter breeze.

The squirrel deep in the hollow tree
Inside his personal dray,
  He waits for the coming warmth
  Of early springtime days.

The dormouse, a tiny rodent
So small he fits in a cup,
  Even when it is warmer
  Reluctantly wakes up.

Deep in an Arctic cave
A polar bear all white,
  Her cuddly cubs, pure as snow
  Will emerge into the light.

But it's not so with man
They, can't slow their heart-rate,
  Such a shame they can't snuggle up
  And through the winter hibernate.

I Am Hurting Inside

My cat, Sparky is no more
He of the fluffy ginger tail,
And bright, round eyes emerald
    He could cry a mighty wail.

The loudest purr one could hear
He would curl up at my feet,
With claws outstretched, I dreaded
    The wrecking of my seat.

He loved the feather duster
Which he ripped to bits,
Funny to watch, his antics
    Had us all in fits.

I will miss him so very much
I acted to end his pain,
I know it will torment my mind
    When I hear his name again.

I loved his habit of greeting
Constantly running to hide,
But there's a big gap left now
    I'm hurting deep inside.

The Pony Troop

The pony troop surges down the lane
    In a slow, stately trot,
Four abreast, blacks and browns
    Some sweating, shiny and hot.

They all have riders proud
    Young, some overweight,
Yet we see they obey the rules
    And always shut the gate.

Some ponies nibble the grass
    That on the wayside grows,
Lush and green, evenly kept
    By regular, careful mows.

The older mares have had enough
    Of carting young, loud know-alls,
But will welcome more tranquillity
    Back in their stable stalls.

Down the lane, the troop moves
    Into a line, one by one,
Tails go up and on the road
    Drop heaps of squashy dung.

They have no clear-up code
    They really do not care,
No apologies for our walking shoes
    That find it steaming there.

The King's Shilling

Why was our sovereign
Called so, when all he paid
To those who enlisted to serve
    Was just a measly shilling!

It really did seem very mean
To pay such a small amount,
To fighting men who died
    In numbers beyond count.

What of their families
Parents, siblings and young,
Left to feed themselves
    And starved one by one.

Did the sovereign care
That poverty ran rife?
Wealth and comfort was his
    All his decadent life.

Better conditions would ensure
Supply of recruits all willing,
To serve their king and country
    By taking the king's shilling.

At last the sovereign realised
He had a solemn duty,
To protect his subjects best he can
    And not hog all the booty.

The Corsair

When the sun has burnt all
The hydrogen from its core,
The worrying question is
    Where will it turn for more?

The inner planets will be consumed
Mercury and Venus too,
Next in line is the Earth
    The home for me and you.

Hydrogen, the source of energy
Burned there for untold years,
Now exhausted, in need of more
    The corsair raid appears.

Small planets do not last for long
As the hydrogen they generate,
Soon burns out rapidly in turn
    They cannot compensate –

For this flaming ball of fire
Approaches day by day,
We will become the next meal
    To feed the bright array.

Where will the sun finish up
As it travels through deep space?
Seeking enough hydrogen
    To adopt a parking place?

A Wartime Child

I was born in the country
    A just before the war, child,
At odds with my parents
That were rarely reconciled.

Air raid sirens constantly
    Wailed warnings to the nation,
German bombers up above
Headed for the power station.

Cold fear would grip my heart
    Hearing the aircraft drone,
I soon learned by the engine's
To tell which were our own.

Running wild like a tom-boy
    Climbing haystacks and trees,
The scars of many accidents
Are visible on my knees.

I lacked siblings and friends
   The discipline was harsh,
Stifling mental exploration
Beyond the farm and yard.

Must go to the chapel
   Attend three times on Sunday,
Never laugh or have a snigger
How I longed to get away.

With the end of the war at last
   I found gainful employment,
The honing of my natural skills
Brought me great enjoyment.

When the Clouds Weep

When a dark storm rages
Disturbing our sleep,
The clouds above are losing
    Raindrops as they weep.

Alas, all is not well
In the high celestial portals,
Thunder claps its spectral hands
    Scaring us mere mortals.

We do not see behind the scenes
Where on the heavenly throne,
Is there a Master of the Universe
    Who reigns forever alone?

An architect of the cosmos
With blueprints truly unique,
Observing from his station
    Why the clouds seem to weep.

Wondering why it is
That his creation below,
Has messed up the planet
    Should it have to go?

The clouds will weep
For such judgement if passed,
Man may have blown his chances
    His species could be outcast.

Thee and Me

We are aright odd couple
Known as thee and me,
Have learned much in our life
By studying history.

We have found ancient works
Of immense interest,
Cannot fault the old ways
That have proved the best.

Life was simple years ago
Everyone in their place,
Contented in their way of life
Taken at a slower pace.

What of thee and me?
Near the end of our road,
We have earned good times
Long overdue and owed.

Fun and games betwixt us two
Laughter rocks us both with glee,
Like kids we find amusement
Where others do not see.

There have been times of stress
When we doubted to get through,
The inner strength in each of us
Has shown what we can do.

Down the Ages

Down the ages has passed a story
    Of a child born long ago,
Who left his home in glory
    To dwell with us below.

Some say it was in December
    This event took place,
In a humble Jewish stable
    As the inn had no space.

It is said he was the son of God
    Sent to redeem our sins,
A sacrifice, an example
    That love always wins.

He grew up to be a man
    With all of mans weakness,
Gathered a large following
    Practising his creed of meekness.

Whatever was done to him
    Very few can deny,
He is the king of heaven
    His empire's up on high.

The Carousel of Fate

Round and round, too fast, spins
Our life, a giant roulette wheel,
Taking lots, giving little
    A beguiling means to steal.

Will it land on black or red?
Where lays the stake
Punters gather round
    Waiting for their fate.

Not only gambling, the carousel
Rotates our life away,
None know what lies ahead
    Be it pleasure or dismay.

The carousel of fate
Our destiny decides,
All we try to do
    Is most tightly hog-tied.

There is but one question
Can we stop the turns?
The carousel cannot be halted
    However much we yearn.

The Restive Spirit

$\mathcal{T}$he Christmas spirit hung around
Not knowing where to go,
    The festival itself had passed
Without a flake of snow.

Friends and family had gathered
Stuffed themselves, indulged in fights,
    The restive spirit knew it was time
To vanish into the night.

It had been a big disaster
This festive holiday break,
    Greed had reigned supreme
Peace on earth, just a fake.

So the spirit roamed
One end of earth to the other,
    Nowhere he could call home
Next year he won't be bothered.

He would give the earth a miss
Seek another planet's embrace,
    There he might strike lucky
Find a welcoming place.

Amongst the multitude of stars
The restive spirit crossed,
    Just one planet in the universe
Could stop him being lost.

Guardians of the Fields

Sporting a magnificent mantle
Of verdant, fresh, young shoots,
Facing the cruel biting winds
    Shaking them down to the roots.

The hedgerows stands firm and strong
Their role they will not yield,
Sheltering plants and the wildlife
    The guardians of the fields.

In the lee of the wind
Inside the thick hedgerow,
Home to tiny jenny wren
    And the hedge sparrow.

The hedgerows have endured
Since man first farmed the fields,
Diverse crops, so reliant on
    The hedgerow's total shield.

We must not grub up
The protection they provide,
Leave them thriving there
    Growing green, thick, and wide.

Tears of a Clown

He dresses up and acts the goat
The gaudy circus clown,
Everybody laughs especially
    When the water bucket's thrown.

But underneath all the hype
Buried in the vivid glitter,
Lives a real wistful, man
    A lonesome, out of place critter.

They all laugh at him
None see the tears of a clown,
His heart belongs to a lady
    And on his sleeve is shown.

She will not give him a glance
And so knowing she's so near,
When the acts are over
    He dissolves in tears.

He only wants friendship
A companion to share his life,
He hardly dares to hope
    One day she'll be his wife.

In the circus big-top
His lady's fallen from up high,
His chance to reassure her
    On him she can rely.

Cousin of the Snail?

Computer's playing up today
       It's on another go-slow,
The websites will not open
       Who can blame the snow?

It can have no effect
       On the performance crawl,
Cousin of the snail, designed
       To drive you up the wall.

When it finally deigns
       To go to a working mode,
Prolonged time of waiting
       Causes you to explode.

Even medical computers
       Have been known to fail,
It seems they've been infected
       By the cousin of the snail.

Why can't it be simple
       Using notes and telephones,
Messages and conversation
       Will avoid frustrations moans.

Supposedly to aid communication
       Electronic, speedy e-mail,
We end up waiting ages
       For this cousin of the snail.

Life's Jumble Sale

*L*ife is a mixture of chances
Just like a jumble sale,
Will we get a bargain
    Or miserably fail?

We put our trust in others
A very big mistake,
A constant gauntlet of risks
    We are forced to take.

Most trusted persons
Will always let you down,
Very few integrity prove
    Never, the first time round.

So, how to sort out the best
In life's jumbled tale?
A hard task to execute
    When every-things for sale.

We do not have the time
To carry out knowledgeable search,
Most of the offered items
    Are useless, shoddy or worse.

In this assorted market
We should not just stop,
By faith and wise judgement
    We can come out on top.

The Red Mist

When tempers snap control is lost
'Tis said the red mist descends,
The quickest and most rapid route
    To lose sight of friends.

Many crimes have been committed
By total lack of discipline,
Some due to drugs or drink
    Addiction's road to ruin.

A knife flashes rapidly
The red mist has descended,
For the unlucky recipient
    A life so quickly ended.

A bullet has the same result
Opponent has little chance,
The gun, a means of sending
    Death by just a glance.

It's all about sticking to
The creeds we comprehend,
Take control, avert the danger
    Of the mists that descend.

The Candle of the Night

We have the sun in the morning
Beaming gold and bright,
At night, the moon gently shines
As a candle of the night.

It does not flare or flicker
This light, cold and ghostly,
A guide for all lost travellers
Just bright enough to see.

To have the moon at night
In all its many forms,
A candle soft and luminous
Shining until morn.

When the moon is full
The sky's a wondrous sight,
So completely dominated
By this lunar candle bright.

We are so very grateful
For these lanterns of the sky,
Sun of gold, warms the heart
Silver moon gliding high.

There's such magic in moonbeams
Firmly coupled with romance,
For with the candle of the night
We still become entranced.

The Mighty Vikings

The Vikings were ingenious
At keeping themselves afloat,
Their designs well demonstrated
    In their beautiful longboats.

Sleek and fast in the water
With the prow rising up high,
Square sails set to catch the wind
    So over the ocean can fly.

Navigating by the stars
They went for many leagues,
To lands undiscovered
    Curiosity to intrigue.

Raiders by nature
The mighty Vikings fought,
At every stopping point
    Slaughter and terror brought.

The humble inhabitants
Of the nearby villages,
Were subject to constant
    Robbery, rape and pillages.

These people had no defence
Against the men of the waves,
The mighty Vikings captors
    Deported them as slaves.

March Wind

The March wind ran out of breath
  From blowing far too long,
Across mountain, sea and plain
  Gusting bleak and strong.

He had huffed and puffed
  From morning until dark,
His energy was running low
  Just not enough to start.

Now the wind must slumber
  Regenerate his strength,
Lots of gales it must start
  Many a blast at length.

Will he blow away the old wood
  That clings to the trees?
Or will he wait for just a while
  And roar when he does please.

He clears away the rubbish
  Thrown down by careless hands,
Scattered, it flies up high
  To dance before it lands.

Hither and thither round the streets
  These flying marionettes,
Carried away aloft
  Like whirling demented pets.

That Look

We all dread the consequences
　　When that look flashed in his eyes,
Uncontrolled, impending violence
Defying to be analysed.

We know he would suddenly explode
　　Hitting, punching, lashing,
Head banged on the wall
Furniture crashing.

It becomes so difficult
　　To describe the fear,
Paralysing us absolutely
When his temper rears.

Police do not consider
　　Domestic violence to be a crime,
Meaning he can indulge in
His beatings anytime.

It takes great courage
　　To escape such a trap,
To make a brand new start
Flounder without a map.

Once the break is made
　　Life can begin again,
He just was not worth it
Years wasted, of love in vain.

Written to encourage victims to change their lives.

Wondrous Things

I lay on the hard baked ground
Thinking of wondrous things,
The sky, a clear azure blue
　　Around me a skylark sings.

I wonder who ordained the birds
And caused them so to sing,
Was it God of the universe
　　Who gave them their beating wings?

On the edge of the ploughed field
Blooms speedwell and red pimpernel,
In silent homage to the God
　　If only they could tell –

How magic is the seasons' course
From spring right through to fall,
It is obvious to the dumbest mind
　　It's no accident at all.

So I gaze up in deepest thought
Seeing no clouds in the sky,
The sun gently heats the earth
    Where in warmth I sleepily lie.

Now I must arouse myself
The sun has moved around,
It is time I stirred my stumps
    And got up off the ground.

I walked quite slowly home
Having nothing much to say,
I'll get a right telling off
    For idling half the day.

Realms of Fantasy

Into the realms of fantasy
    Drifts the mind when half asleep,
Fairytale adventures blend with
Dark denizens of the deep.

Fantasising can bring pleasure
    Sometimes the most dreadful fears,
In the morning, with daylight
The whole lot disappears.

Shining knights in armour bright
    Champion maidens in dire need,
Ending up inevitably, with them
Riding on his steed.

Romancing, dreaming of love
    All part of fantasy's realms,
The danger is, it seems so real
With a dreamer at the helm.

A ship adrift on a sea of thoughts
    Can never find its home port,
Always, in morning light discovers
In an endless loop is caught.

Reality may seem so harsh
    But will remove any doubt,
Dreaming, like tinted glasses,
A rosy world throughout.

Priorities

There are many times in life
When priorities come to the fore,
    In the welfare of home
And family health to restore.

Our loved ones must stay on top
Fit and well to remain,
    Able to enjoy their leisure
Their lifestyle to maintain.

Looking out for family
Priority number one must be,
    Rather than drink or smoking
Which carries such penalties.

Common sense and concern
Must come before all other,
    Cravings for tobacco
Wine, food or a lover.

We must keep a grip, on life
One must do it right,
    One must be strong willed
And keep true values in sight.

Leap Year Lady

The twenty ninth of February
Occurs once in four years,
A birthday on that day
    Especially blessed appears.

True age can be divided by four
Making you forever young,
Loved and cherished always
    By all you are among.

Being a wife and mother
You are a Leap Year Lady,
This poem is dedicated
    To you our busy Hayley.

You buzz round all day long
Looking after your family,
A charming natural mother
    A lady of quality.

Your husband knows this is true
And appreciates your worth,
Your bubbly sensitivity was
    Apparent from your birth.

Dedicated to my daughter-in-law.

Valentine 2011 (II)

Once again it is my task
　　To pen a few short lines,
In appreciation of my husband dear
　　My wonderful Valentine.

He takes the greatest care
　　Of me, although a pain,
How I wish I could improve
　　My mobility to regain.

I try my best to please him
　　So afraid to fail,
One thing that is certain
　　My love will not go stale.

There are a few occasions
　　When our opinions vary,
I like to give up, rather than
　　Let matters become too hairy.

My love for this man is firm,
　　Passionate, hot and strong,
The bond that binds me now
　　Will carry me along.

Another year, another effort
　　An easy simple rhyme,
Just to say I treasure you
　　My beloved Valentine.

There can be no doubt at all
　　I truly, deeply care,
For you my dear husband
　　Love is in the air.

How Does He Know?

A bunny visits our garden
Daily on the hour of nine,
The question then arises
　　How does he know the time?

Every morning he is seen
Nibbling, running around,
Eating on the varied bits
　　That on the grass are found.

He tries all sorts of food
Not usual for his kind,
Bread, cake, meat scraps
　　Anything he can find.

He enjoys basking by the fence
Close to where he has a hole,
The cleaning of his whiskers
　　Seems to be his goal.

He has a dark brown tail
Not like the general white,
His feet, cream in colour
　　Visible in his flight.

He may come back again
More than once a day,
Foraging in the grass
　　'Til it's time to run away.

Sometimes

*L*ife can be so difficult
    Struggling to get things right,
It's just as if there is a curse
    Or some other kind of blight.

Sometimes it seems if at last
    The matter will be resolved,
But the plague therein lurking
    Drops me down the hole.

I often feel like giving up
    Try finding another way,
Sometimes I find the odds too great
    Which fills me with dismay.

However I am the terrier breed
    Which always hangs on,
Pulling, tugging, pulling more
    'Til the problem's gone.

I believe in trying hard
    Whatever be the task,
My face reveals the strain
    More than I can mask.

Some folks like solving puzzles
    Some prefer DIY,
Sometimes I log on the computer
    But is it a covert spy?

What Will They Think

What will they think of me
 When I am no longer here?
Will they one day come to feel
 I am still hovering near?

Demands were piled on me
Coming from right and left,
In time will they see?
 Will they be bereft?

Life treated me so hard
And left me very low,
I still watch over them
 See them rushing to and fro.

I tried to do the right thing
In every troubled case.
Working so very hard
 To keep title and place.

My family, all a part,
I truly loved each one,
I gave them all I could
    But no more when I'm gone.

They will never understand
My personal agony,
Giving up my position
    To save the company.

Will they always remember
And fond memories keep?
Bearing in mind consciously
    My still waters ran deep.

Thoughts

I have many a feeling and thought,
Written many poems to date,
Seeking out the truth of life
  Of destiny and of fate.

I have tried to share my views
On subjects wide and far,
My feelings and strong beliefs
  On earth and in the stars.

I want to leave a legacy
For my descendants to digest,
I'm only an amateur
  Pale amongst the rest.

I believe in being kind
Towards my fellow man,
Extending a helping hand
  Assisting where I can.

I've revealed my inner thoughts
Pouring out my heart and soul,
Covering where I could,
    All subjects from pole to pole.

I firmly believe in goodness
Apparent in just a few,
A shining quality of worth,
    Lighting, their whole life through.

Friction and wars continue
Spreading like the plague,
Will we ever see true peace?
    Upon this worldly stage.